EN

# ENGLAND

*A Collection of the Poetry of Place*

*Edited by*
**A. N. WILSON**

ELAND • LONDON

This arrangement and commentary
© A. N. Wilson

ISBN   978 1 906011 21 5

First published in October 2008 by Eland Publishing Ltd,
61 Exmouth Market, Clerkenwell, London EC1R 4QL

Pages designed and typeset by Antony Gray
Cover image: The Weald of Kent, *c.*1827–8
(watercolour and gouache on paper)
Samuel Palmer (1805–81)
Centre for British Art,
Paul Mellon Collection, Yale, USA
Printed and bound in Spain by
GraphyCems, Navarra

# CONTENTS

ONE  PREAMBLE                                    9

TWO  ELEGIES                                     11

THREE  WARRIOR RACE                              27

FOUR  ALBION'S BEAUTIES                          37

FIVE  PLATONIC ENGLAND                           69

SIX  WRECKAGE                                    79

SEVEN  THE INTERSECTION OF
       THE TIMELESS MOMENT                       87

EIGHT  THE PEOPLE OF ENGLAND                     97

       Acknowledgements                          108

       Index of first lines                      109

       Index of poem titles                      111

       Index of poets                            112

ENGLAND is no more. That is why this is a good time to celebrate it, mourn it, sing elegies for it. This is not the place to analyse why, or when, the disappearance happened. World wars, tarmacadamed roads, the influence of the United States of America, their music and their foods, the growth of commerce, and the growth of belief in growth; large numbers of immigrants from former colonies; shame at having possessed the colonies, regret at their loss, or a mingling of the two emotions – all these no doubt contributed to what we all know. We stand in what appears to be remote meadow land, and hear not the song bird, but the distant roar of motor traffic. We attend cathedral worship, and hear, not the words which have echoed in those stones since the reign of the first Elizabeth, but alien, jarring words, injurious to faith as well as repellent to the ear. We are of a generation that has never seen an old market town unmarred by thoughtless town planning, intrusive road signs, tactless functional building, and aggressive emendations to the doors and window frames of buildings which have stood since the time of George III. We have watched those characters familiar in fact as well as in nursery rhyme – the butcher, the baker, the candlestick maker – replaced by out-of-town shopping malls, and supermarkets. We have seen corn exchanges turned into mosques and old parsonages made into the second homes of hedge-fund managers.

The England of our grandparents, then, is no more. And, what is more, the Union is unlikely to survive. In the eighteenth, nineteenth and early-to-mid twentieth century, the word 'English' denoted not merely the shared language, but also the shared identity of the inhabitants of the archipelago, even if some of those inhabitants were Manx, Men of Sark, Irish, Scotchmen or Welsh. Now, 'England' and 'English' mean something rather diminished. Scotch Nationalists will create their own independent nation state. The Welsh, with their own assembly, will presumably occupy a position of some ambiguity. England will be the rump.

The poetry in this book is not about the political entity which will survive these acts of political jiggery-pokery. It is about what Samuel Taylor Coleridge (and Geoffrey Hill, imitating him) called Platonic England.

If some of the poems and verses which are found here strike a jarring note in our ear, this is caused not by their lack of euphony, but by the fact that we have moved so far from the mindset which created them, from the spiritual world of hearers who learnt them and made them part of their inner lives. For, it is safe to say that almost every word which I have gathered up in this book (with the exception of the most modern) was once known by heart by any literate Englishman or Englishwoman. If they seem strange today, that is a sign of how far we have travelled from home.

# ONE

# PREAMBLE

Daniel Defoe, best known today for his story of a man marooned upon a desert island, *Robinson Crusoe*, found himself marooned by fate upon the island of Great Britain. He was by nature a nonconformist. His body lies with those other great English Nonconformists Isaac Watts and William Blake in Bunhill Fields. These reflections on the 'true-born Englishman' resonate interestingly today.

Satire, be kind, and draw a silent veil,
Thy native England's vices to conceal;
Or, if that task's impossible to do,
At least be just, and show her virtues too;
Too great the first, alas! the last too few.
England, unknown, as yet, unpeopled lay,–
Happy, had she remained so to this day,
And not to every nation been a prey …
The Romans first with Julius Caesar came,
Including all the nations of that name,
Gauls, Greeks, and Lombards; and by computation,
Auxiliaries or slaves of every nation.
When Hengist, Saxons; Danes with Sweno came,
In search of plunder, not in search of fame.
Scots, Picts, and Irish from the Hibernian shore;
And conquering William brought the Normans o'er.
All these their barbarous offspring left behind,

The dregs of armies, they of all mankind;
Blended with Britons, who before were here,
Of whom the Welsh have blessed the character.

Thus from a mixture of all kinds began,
That heterogeneous thing, an Englishman:
In eager rapes, and furious lust begot,
Betwixt a painted Briton and a Scot:
Whose gendering offspring quickly learned to bow,
And yoke their heifers to the Roman plough;
From whence a mongrel half-bred race there came,
With neither name nor nation, speech nor fame,
In whose hot veins new mixtures quickly ran,
Infused betwixt a Saxon and a Dane;
While their rank daughters, to their parents just,
Received all nations with promiscuous lust.
This nauseous brood directly did contain
The well-extracted blood of Englishmen …

The Scot, Pict, Briton, Roman, Dane submit,
And with the English Saxon all unite:
And these the mixture have so close pursued,
The very name and memory's subdued;
No Roman now, no Briton, does remain;
Wales strove to separate, but strove in vain:
The silent nations undistinguished fall,
And Englishman's the common name for all.
Fate jumbled them together, God knows how;
Whate'er they were, they're true-born English now.

From *The True-Born Englishman*
by DANIEL DEFOE (1659/61?–1731)

# TWO

# ELEGIES

John of Gaunt's speech in *Richard II* is more often remembered, by those who committed it to memory during childhood, as a celebration of 'This other Eden, demi-Paradise'. But perhaps one of the features of our English Paradise is that it has always been a Paradise Lost. John of Gaunt saw England let out 'like to a tenement or pelting farm'. For those of us who feel that England has gone to the dogs, it is salutary to be reminded that it has been going to the dogs at least since the fourteenth century.

GAUNT
Methinks I am a prophet new inspir'd,
And thus expiring do foretell of him:
His rash fierce blaze of riot cannot last;
For violent fires soon burn out themselves;
Small showers last long, but sudden storms are short;
He tires betimes that spurs too fast betimes;
With eager feeding food doth choke the feeder:
Light vanity, insatiate cormorant,
Consuming means, soon preys upon itself.
This royal throne of kings, this scepter'd isle,
This earth of majesty, this seat of Mars,
This other Eden, demi-paradise,
This fortress built by Nature for herself
Against infection and the hand of war,
This happy breed of men, this little world,

This precious stone set in the silver sea,
Which serves it in the office of a wall,
Or as a moat defensive to a house,
Against the envy of less happier lands,
This blessed plot, this earth, this realm, this England,
This nurse, this teeming womb of royal kings,
Fear'd by their breed and famous by their birth,
Renowned for their deeds as far from home,–
For Christian service and true chivalry,–
As is the sepulchre in stubborn Jewry
Of the world's ransom, blessed Mary's Son:
This land of such dear souls, this dear, dear land,
Dear for her reputation, through the world,
Is now leas'd out,– I die pronouncing it,–
Like to a tenement, or pelting farm:
England, bound in with the triumphant sea,
Whose rocky shore beats back the envious siege
Of watery Neptune, is now bound in with shame,
With inky blots, and rotten parchment bonds:
That England, that was wont to conquer others
Hath made a shameful conquest of itself.
Ah! Would the scandal vanish with my life,
How happy then were my ensuing death.

From *Richard II* by WILLIAM SHAKESPEARE (1564–1616)

If anyone wanted to experience the shock of England's demise, they could not do better than to contrast a journey by Virgin Trains or First Great Western and the sleepy railway journey evoked by Edward Thomas when his train pulled up at Adlestrop before the First World War. Such stations actually survived in England until the 1960s. But the machinations of Harold Macmillan and Harold Beeching, who tore up thousands of miles of railway track, and closed the branch lines, drove the English to the autobahn-styled motorway, and the traffic jam. And thereby was lost, not merely a way of travelling, but also part of Platonic England.

## Adlestrop

Yes, I remember Adlestrop –
The name, because one afternoon
Of heat the express-train drew up there
Unwontedly. It was late June.

The steam hissed. Someone cleared his throat.
No one left and no one came
On the bare platform. What I saw
Was Adlestrop – only the name

And willows, willow-herb, and grass,
And meadowsweet, and haycocks dry,
No whit less still and lonely fair
Than the high cloudlets in the sky.

And for that minute a blackbird sang
Close by, and round him, mistier,
Farther and farther, all the birds
Of Oxfordshire and Gloucestershire.

EDWARD THOMAS (1878–1917)

*Puck of Pook's Hill* allows some Sussex children to revisit the past of their patch of English soil. They see, and speak with, the Roman legionnaires, with the Norman occupier taking possession of a Saxon manor, with the Elizabethans who looked out to the Channel, determined to resist the threat of the Spanish Armada. Rudyard Kipling brilliantly used Shakespeare's Puck, or Robin Goodfellow, as the medium for these time travels. Here is his song.

See you the ferny ride that steals
Into the oak-woods far?
O that was whence they hewed the keels
That rolled to Trafalgar.

And mark you where the ivy clings
To Bayham's mouldering walls?
O there we cast the stout railings
That stand around St. Paul's.

See you the dimpled track that runs
All hollow through the wheat?
O that was where they hauled the guns
That smote King Philip's fleet.

(Out of the Weald, the secret Weald,
Men sent in ancient years,
The horse-shoes red at Flodden Field,
The arrows at Poitiers!)

See you our little mill that clacks,
So busy by the brook?
She has ground her corn and paid her tax
Ever since Domesday Book.

See you our silly woods of oak,
And the dread ditch beside?

O that was where the Saxons broke
On the day that Harold died.

See you the windy levels spread
About the gates of Rye?
O that was where the Northmen fled,
When Alfred's ships came by.

See you our pastures wide and lone,
Where the red oxen browse?
O there was a City thronged and known,
Ere London boasted a house.

And see you, after rain, the trace
Of mound and ditch and wall?
O that was a Legion's camping-place,
When Caesar sailed from Gaul.

And see you marks that show and fade,
Like shadows on the Downs?
O they are the lines the Flint Men made,
To guard their wondrous towns.

Trackway and Camp and City lost,
Salt Marsh where now is corn–
Old Wars, old Peace, old Arts that cease,
And so was England born!

She is not any common Earth,
Water or wood or air,
But Merlin's Isle of Gramarye,
Where you and I will fare!

From *Puck of Pook's Hill* by
RUDYARD KIPLING (1865–1936)

Kipling, who had been born in Lahore, had an intense relationship with England, strengthened by the poignant knowledge of exile. His Sussex neighbour Hilaire Belloc was a very different man. Whereas Kipling was an arch-Imperialist, Belloc was a Liberal Radical MP, who used to say of the British Empire, 'I hate the name and I hate the thing'. Belloc was half French, and had been born in Paris. He did his national service in the French army. Perhaps this explained his half-exile's love of England, and his elegist's sense of desolation, captured in this exquisite lyric, written long before the First World War.

## Ha'nacker Mill

Sally is gone that was so kindly
   Sally is gone from Ha'nacker Hill.
And the Briar grows ever since then so blindly
   And ever since then the clapper is still,
   And the sweeps have fallen from Ha'nacker Mill.

Ha'nacker Hill is in Desolation:
   Ruin a-top and a field unploughed.
And Spirits that call on a fallen nation
   Spirits that loved her calling aloud:
   Spirits abroad in a windy cloud.

Spirits that call and no one answers;
   Ha'nacker's down and England's done.
Wind and Thistle for pipe and dancers
   And never a ploughman under the Sun.
   Never a ploughman. Never a one.

HILAIRE BELLOC (1870–1953)

Whatever quickened the demise of Old England, hindsight shows that the destruction began with the First World War. We still, in our annual recollection of the massacres which wiped out millions of young lives in the years 1914–18, repeat Laurence Binyon's words, though many people only know the lines from the fourth verse, without a knowledge of the entire, very fine, poem. I conclude this section of the book with some poems which reflect the catastrophe of that war. Rupert Brooke's 'The Soldier' became a classic anthology piece almost as soon as it was written. The hymn 'O Valiant Hearts' is included to remind us of the sentiments felt up to, and beyond, the Second World War, by many English people, though they are probably not much felt now. Old Thomas Hardy's poem 'Channel Firing' concludes the section. It was written in April 1914, four months before the war actually broke out, and consists of a grim conversation between the skeletons in a Wessex churchyard as they hear gun practice in the channel. The old land, whose memory stretches back beyond the mythical court of King Arthur at Camelot to the mysterious stone circle on Salisbury Plain, is to be shattered in the 'indifferent' twentieth century by those who are 'mad as hatters'.


## The Soldier


If I should die, think only this of me:
    That there's some corner of a foreign field
That is for ever England. There shall be
    In that rich earth a richer dust conceal'd;
A dust whom England bore, shaped, made aware,
    Gave, once, her flowers to love, her ways to roam,
A body of England's, breathing English air.
    Wash'd by the rivers, blest by suns of home.

And think, this heart, all evil shed away,
    A pulse in the eternal mind, no less
    Gives somewhere back the thoughts by England given;
Her sights and sounds; dreams happy as her day;
    And laughter, learnt of friends; and gentleness,
    In hearts at peace, under an English heaven.

RUPERT BROOKE (1887–1915)

## O Valiant Hearts

O valiant hearts who to your glory came
Through dust of conflict and through battle flame;
    Tranquil you lie, your knightly virtue proved,
    Your memory hallowed in the land you loved.

    Proudly you gathered, rank on rank, to war
    As who had heard God's message from afar;
    All you had hoped for, all you had, you gave,
To save mankind – yourselves you scorned to save.

Splendid you passed, the great surrender made;
    Into the light that nevermore shall fade;
    Deep your contentment in that blest abode,
    Who wait the last clear trumpet call of God.

    Long years ago, as earth lay dark and still,
        Rose a loud cry upon a lonely hill,
    While in the frailty of our human clay,
Christ, our Redeemer, passed the self same way.

Still stands His Cross from that dread hour to this,
    Like some bright star above the dark abyss;
    Still, through the veil, the Victor's pitying eyes
        Look down to less our lesser Calvaries.

These were His servants, in His steps they trod,
Following through death, the martyred Son of God:
    Victor, he rose; victorious too shall rise
    They who have drunk His cup of sacrifice.

O risen Lord, O Shepherd of our dead,
Whose cross has brought them and Whose staff has led,
    In glorious hope their proud and sorrowing land
    Commits her children to Thy gracious hand.

SIR JOHN ARKWRIGHT (1872–1954)


## For the Fallen

With proud thanksgiving, a mother for her children,
England mourns for her dead across the sea.
Flesh of her flesh they were, spirit of her spirit,
Fallen in the cause of the free.

Solemn the drums thrill: Death august and royal
Sings sorrow up into immortal spheres.
There is music in the midst of desolation
And a glory that shines upon our tears.

They went with songs to the battle, they were young,
Straight of limb, true of eye, steady and aglow.
They were staunch to the end against odds uncounted,
They fell with their faces to the foe.

They shall grow not old, as we that are left grow old:
Age shall not weary them, nor the years condemn.
At the going down of the sun and in the morning
We will remember them.

They mingle not with their laughing comrades again;
They sit no more at familiar tables of home;
They have no lot in our labour of the day-time;
They sleep beyond England's foam.

But where our desires are and our hopes profound,
Felt as a well-spring that is hidden from sight,
To the innermost heart of their own land they are known
As the stars are known to the Night;

As the stars that shall be bright when we are dust,
Moving in marches upon the heavenly plain,
As the stars that are starry in the time of our darkness.
To the end, to the end, they remain.

LAURENCE BINYON (1869–1943)


## Channel Firing

That night your great guns, unawares,
Shook all our coffins as we lay,
And broke the chancel window-squares,
We thought it was the Judgment-day

And sat upright. While drearisome
Arose the howl of wakened hounds:
The house let fall the altar-crumb,
The worms drew back into the mounds,

The glebe cow drooled. Till God called, 'No
It's gunnery practice out at sea
Just as before you went below;
The world is as it used to be:

'All nations striving strong to make
Red war yet redder. Mad as hatters
They do no more for Christés sake
Than you who are helpless in such matters.

'That this is not the judgment-hour
For some of them's a blessed thing,
For if it were they'd have to scour
Hell's floor for so much threatening …

'Ha, ha. It will be warmer when
I blow the trumpet (if indeed
I ever do; for you are men,
And rest eternal sorely need.)'

So down we lay again. 'I wonder,
Will the world ever saner be,'
Said one, 'than when He sent us under
In our indifferent century!'

And many a skeleton shook his head.
'Instead of preaching forty year,'
My neighbour Parson Thirdly said,
'I wish I had stuck to pipes and beer.'

Again the guns disturbed the hour,
Roaring their readiness to avenge,
And far inland as Stourton Tower,
And Camelot, and starlit Stonehenge.

THOMAS HARDY (1840–1928)

John Betjeman's elegy for rural Middlesex is robust enough to enjoy, or half enjoy, the world of Elaine which replaces it. The poem is dense in allusion. Drene is a shampoo, a bobby-soxer was a teenager; a Windsmoor was a coat. Murray Posh and Lupin Pooter were the two silly young men in Betjeman's favourite *Diary of a Nobody*.

## Middlesex

Gaily into Ruislip Gardens
    Runs the red electric train,
With a thousand Ta's and Pardon's
    Daintily alights Elaine;
Hurries down the concrete station
With a frown of concentration,
Out into the outskirt's edges
Where a few surviving hedges
Keep alive our last Elysium – rural Middlesex again.

Well cut Windsmoor flapping lightly,
    Jacqmar scarf of mauve and green
Hiding hair which, Friday nightly,
    Delicately drowns in Drene;
Fair Elaine the bobby-soxer,
Fresh-complexioned with Innoxa,
Gains the garden – father's hobby –
Hangs her Windsmoor in the lobby,
Settles down to sandwich supper and the television screen.

Gentle Brent, I used to know you
    Wandering Wembley-wards at will,

Now what change your waters show you
   In the meadowlands you fill!
Recollect the elm-trees misty
   And the footpaths climbing twisty
Under cedar-shaded palings,
Low laburnum-leaned-on railings,
Out of Northolt on and upward to the heights of Harrow hill.

Parish of enormous hayfields
   Perivale stood all alone,
And from Greenford scent of mayfields
   Most enticingly was blown
Over market gardens tidy,
Taverns for the *bona fide*,
Cockney anglers, cockney shooters,
Murray Poshes, Lupin Pooters
Long in Kensal Green and Highgate silent under soot and stone.

JOHN BETJEMAN (1906–84)

And two more elegies – A. E. Housman's exquisite lyric from *A Shropshire Lad*, and, from Evelyn Waugh's *Brideshead Revisited*, the ruminations of the dying Marquess of Marchmain. In his baroque, eighteenth-century house, he meditates upon an aristocratic family, its rootedness to a particular area of England, its connectedness with England's past. Waugh makes it into a prose-poem of startling beauty.

We live long in our family and marry late. Seventy-three is no great age. Aunt Julia, my father's aunt, lived to be eighty-eight, born and died there, never married, saw the fire on beacon hill for the battle of Trafalgar, always called it 'the New House'; that was the name they had for it in the nursery and in the fields when unlettered men had long memories. You can see where the old house stood near the village church; they call the field 'Castle Hill', Horlick's field where the ground's uneven and half of it is waste, nettle, and brier in hollows too deep for ploughing. They dug to the foundations to carry the stone for the new house; the house that was a century old when Aunt Julia was born. Those were our roots in the waste hollows of Castle Hill, in the brier and nettle; among the tombs in the old church and the chantry where no clerk sings.

Aunt Julia knew the tombs, cross-legged knight and doubleted earl, marquis like a Roman senator, limestone, alabaster, and Italian marble; tapped the escutcheons with her ebony cane, made the casque ring over old Sir Roger. We were knights then, barons since Agincourt, the larger honours came with the Georges. They came the last and they'll go the first; the barony goes on. When all of you are dead Julia's son will be called by the name his fathers bore before the fat days; the days of wool shearing and the wide corn lands, the days of growth and building, when the marshes were drained and the waste land brought under the plough, when one built the house, his son added the dome, his son spread the wings and dammed the river. Aunt Julia watched them build the fountain; it was old before it came here, weathered two

hundred years by the suns of Naples, brought by man-o'-war
in the days of Nelson. Soon the fountain will be dry till the
rain fills it, setting the fallen leaves afloat in the basin; and
over the lakes the reeds will spread and close.

EVELYN WAUGH (1903–66)


## from *A Shropshire Lad*

On Wenlock Edge the wood's in trouble;
    His forest fleece the Wrekin heaves;
The gale, it plies the saplings double,
    And thick on Severn snow the leaves.

'Twould blow like this through holt and hanger
    When Uricon the city stood;
'Tis the old wind in the old anger,
    But then it threshed another wood.

Then, 'twas before my time, the Roman
    At yonder heaving hill would stare:
The blood that warms an English yeoman,
    The thoughts that hurt him, they were there.

There, like the wind through woods in riot,
    Through him the gale of life blew high;
The tree of man was never quiet:
    Then 'twas the Roman, now 'tis I.

The gale, it plies the saplings double,
    It blows so hard, 'twill soon be gone:
To-day the Roman and his trouble
    Are ashes under Uricon.

A. E. HOUSMAN (1859–1936)

# THREE

# WARRIOR RACE

For the last couple of generations, wars have been noises off – in the Balkans, in Africa, in the Middle East and the Far East. The rights and wrongs of these conflicts can be discussed in newspaper articles, and in conversation. Sometimes, as in the case of the Suez invasion in 1956, or the Iraq war waged by President George W. Bush and Tony Blair, such wars excite passionately differing views in the home country. But views are not the same as the experience of war, and the threat of invasion.

The generation which is now dying out lived with the likelihood, fading to possibility, of enemy invasion; and the experience, not of the occasional terrorist explosion, as has occurred in our time, but of nightly storms of bombs, which turned English cities to infernos. (The retaliation upon German cities was yet more terrible.)

There were some who looked back on the Second World War as a time of unrelieved unhappiness, and among these, obviously, are those who lost brothers, husbands, lovers and parents in the war. Yet the ever-presence of danger, and the opportunities for noble and gallant behaviour which it afforded, must be part of the reason why so many of the English continued to view the Second World War with nostalgia. You only have to spend half an hour in the company of those who lived through it as grown-ups to realise how deeply many of them enjoyed it. The poems which follow do not belong to the Second World War. Of all the great wars in English history, it produced the lowest crop of memorable verse. Rather, this section contains poetry representative of the warlike quality of England and the English. It begins with William Cowper's splendid verses on Boadicea. I first heard it being recited by my father (born 1902) and by his sister Elizabeth, my favourite aunt, who was about ten years his senior. They both lived to see the England of Margaret Thatcher (a figure they were old fashioned enough to regard with a mixture of admiration and misgiving – admiration for her courage, misgiving, given her position, for her sex). Hence the frequency with which the figure of Boadicea came to their minds.

Alfred Tennyson's 'Hands All Round!' reflects the possibility of national invasion by the French in 1852. Sophisticates at the time, and since, have smiled at conservative reminders that England has actually been free of tyrants, and gaols where the inmates were tortured, for rather longer than Bourbon Naples. (That is what Tennyson is alluding to in 'wronged Poerio's noisome den'; Carlo Poerio, who suffered in these dungeons, alerted English liberals such as Gladstone and Tennyson to the sheer nastiness of the regime which still prevailed in Naples. Nor was the awakening entirely smug: it led to Gladstone's realisation that he was in no position to criticise Naples while Ireland languished.)

The speech of Henry V before Harfleur was no doubt learnt by heart by the sort of public schoolboys captured in Clifton-educated Henry Newbolt's 'Vitaï Lampada'. Sir Francis Hastings Doyle, in his poem 'The Private of the Buffs', reminds us that it was not only the public school hearties whose behaviour, loutish in peacetime, could turn to heroism in times of war. The reference to the 'dusky Indians' who 'whine and kneel' is an example of what was mentioned in the introduction to this book – a jarring note which reminds us of the difference between our thought processes and those of our forebears.

# Boadicea

When the British warrior Queen,
    Bleeding from the Roman rods,
Sought with an indignant mien
    Counsel of her country's gods:

Sage beneath the spreading oak
    Sat the Druid, hoary chief,
Ev'ry burning word he spoke
    Full of rage, and full of grief:

'Princess! if our aged eyes
    Weep upon thy matchless wrongs,
'Tis because resentment ties
    All the terrors of our tongues.

'Rome shall perish – write that word
    In the blood that she has spilt;
Perish, hopeless and abhorr'd,
    Deep in ruin as in guilt.

'Rome for empire, far renown'd,
    Tramples on a thousand states;
Soon her pride shall kiss the ground –
    Hark! The Gaul is at her gates!

'Other Romans shall arise,
    Heedless of a soldier's name;
Sounds, not arms, shall win the prize,
    Harmony the path to fame.

'Then the progeny that springs
    From the forests of our land,

Arm'd with thunder, clad with wings,
   Shall a wider world command.

'Regions Caesar never knew
   Thy posterity shall away;
Where his eagles never flew,
   None invincible as they.'

Such the bard's prophetic words
   Pregnant with celestial fire,
Bending, as he swept the chords
   Of his sweet but awful lyre.

She, with all a monarch's pride,
   Felt them in her bosom glow;
Rush'd to battle, fought, and died;
   Dying, hurl'd them at the foe.

'Ruffians, pitiless as proud,
   Heav'n awards the vengeance due:
Empire is on us bestow'd,
   Shame and ruin wait for you.'

WILLIAM COWPER (1731–1800)

## Vitai Lampada

There's a breathless hush in the Close to-night –
Ten to make and the match to win –
A bumping pitch and a blinding light,
    An hour to play and the last man in,
And it's not for the sake of a ribboned coat,
    Or the selfish hope of a season's fame,
But his Captain's hand on his shoulder smote –
'Play up! play up! and play the game!'

The sand of the desert is sodden red ,–
Red with the wreck of a square that broke;–
The Gatling's jammed and the Colonel dead,
    And the regiment blind with dust and smoke.
The river of death has brimmed his banks,
    And England's far, and Honour a name,
But the voice of a schoolboy rallies the ranks:
 'Play up! play up! and play the game!'

This is the word that year by year,
    While in her place the School is set,
Every one of her sons must hear,
    And none that hears it dare forget.
This they all with a joyful mind
    Bear through life like a torch in flame,
And falling fling to the host behind –
'Play up! play up! and play the game!'

HENRY NEWBOLT (1862–1938)

# FROM *Henry V*

Act 3, Scene 1. *France. Before Harfleur.*
*Alarums. Enter* KING HENRY, EXETER, BEDFORD,
GLOUCESTER *and* SOLDIERS, *with scaling ladders.*

KING HENRY:

Once more unto the breach, dear friends, once more;
Or close the wall up with our English dead!
In peace there's nothing so becomes a man
As modest stillness and humility:
But when the blast of war blows in our ears,
Then imitate the action of the tiger;
Stiffen the sinews, summon up the blood,
Disguise fair nature with hard-favour'd rage;
Then lend the eye a terrible aspect;
Let it pry through the portage of the head
Like the brass cannon; let the brow o'erwhelm it
As fearfully as doth a galled rock
O'erhang and jutty his confounded base,
Swill'd with the wild and wasteful ocean.
Now set the teeth and stretch the nostril wide,
Hold hard the breath, and bend up every spirit
To his full height! On, on, you noblest English!
Whose blood is fet from fathers of war-proof;
Fathers that, like so many Alexanders,
Have in these parts from morn till even fought,
And sheath'd their swords for lack of argument.
Dishonour not your mothers; now attest
That those whom you call'd fathers did beget you.
Be copy now to men of grosser blood,

And teach them how to war. And you, good yeomen,
Whose limbs were made in England, show us here
The mettle of your pasture; let us swear
That you are worth your breeding; which I doubt not;
For there is none of you so mean and base
That hath not noble lustre in your eyes.
I see you stand like greyhounds in the slips,
Straining upon the start. The game's afoot:
Follow your spirit; and, upon this charge
Cry 'God for Harry! England and Saint George!'

[*Exeunt. Alarum, and chambers go off*

WILLIAM SHAKESPEARE (1564–1616)


## Hands All Round!

First drink a health, this solemn night,
    A health to England, every guest;
That man's the best cosmopolite,
    Who loves his native country best.
May Freedom's oak for ever live
    With stronger life from day to day;
That man's the true Conservative,
    Who lops the mouldered branch away.
        Hands all round!
        God the tyrant's hope confound!
    To this great cause of freedom drink, my friends,
    And the great name of England round and round.

A health to Europe's honest men!
    Heaven guard them from her tyrants' jails!
From wronged Poerio's noisome den,

From ironed limbs and tortured nails!
We curse the crimes of southern kings,
   The Russian whips and Austrian rods –
We, likewise, have our evil things;
   Too much we make our Ledgers, Gods.
      Yet hands all round!
      God the tyrant's cause confound!
   To Europe's better health we drink, my friends,
   And the great name of England round and round.

What health to France, if France be she,
   Whom martial prowess only charms?
Yet tell her – Better to be free
   Than vanquish all the world in arms.
Her frantic city's flashing heats
   But fire, to blast, the hopes of men.
Why change the titles of your streets?
   You fools, you'll want them all again.
      Yet hands all round!
      God the tyrant's cause confound!
   To France, the wiser France, we drink, my friends,
   And the great name of England round and round.

Gigantic daughter of the West,
   We drink to thee across the flood,
We know thee most, we love thee best,
   For art thou not of British blood?
Should war's mad blast again be blown,
   Permit not thou the tyrant powers
To fight thy mother here alone,
   But let thy broadsides roar with ours.
      Hands all round!
      God the tyrant's cause confound!

To our great kinsmen of the West, my friends,
   And the great name of England round and round.

O rise, our strong Atlantic sons,
   When war against our freedom springs!
O speak to Europe through your guns!
   They *can* be understood by kings.
You must not mix our Queen with those
   That wish to keep their people fools;
Our freedom's foemen are her foes,
   She comprehends the race she rules.
      Hands all round!
      God the tyrant's cause confound!
   To our dear kinsmen of the West, my friends,
And the great cause of freedom round and round.

ALFRED, LORD TENNYSON (1809–92)


## The Private of the Buffs

Last night, among his fellow roughs,
   He jested, quaff'd, and swore;
A drunken private of the Buffs,
   Who never look'd before.
To-day, beneath the foeman's frown,
   He stands in Elgin's place,
Ambassador from Britain's crown
   And type of all her race.

Poor, reckless, rude, low-born, untaught,
   Bewilder'd, and alone,
A heart with English instinct fraught
   He yet can call his own.

35

Aye, tear his body limb from limb,
    Bring cord, or axe, or flame:
He only knows, that not through him
    Shall England come to shame.

Far Kentish hop-fields round him seem'd,
    Like dreams, to come and go;
Bright leagues of cherry-blossom gleam'd,
    One sheet of living snow;
The smoke above his father's door
    In grey soft eddyings hung:
Must he then watch it rise no more,
    Doom'd by himself, so young?

Yes, honour calls! – with strength like steel
    He put the vision by.
Let dusky Indians whine and kneel;
    An English lad must die.
And thus, with eyes that would not shrink,
    With knee to man unbent,
Unfaltering on its dreadful brink,
    To his red grave he went.

Vain, mightiest fleets of iron framed;
    Vain, those all-shattering guns;
Unless proud England keep, untamed,
    The strong heart of her sons.
So, let his name through Europe ring –
    A man of mean estate,
Who died, as firm as Sparta's king,
    Because his soul was great.

SIR FRANCIS HASTINGS DOYLE (1810–88)

# FOUR

# ALBION'S BEAUTIES

What would an English person miss most if compelled to live abroad? The sausages, thought Graham Greene. Byron, in the following extract from *Don Juan*, missed the beer. (By the way, although the Spanish pronounce the name of this lecherous knight 'Don Hwahn', Byron, as his poem shows, anglicised the pronunciation to 'Don Jew-un'.)

### 69

Don Juan, now saw Albion's earliest beauties,
Thy cliffs, *dear* Dover! harbour, and hotel;
Thy custom-house, with all its delicate duties;
Thy waiters running mucks at every bell;
Thy packets, all whose passengers are booties
To those who upon land or water dwell;
And last, not least, to strangers uninstructed,
Thy long, long bills whence nothing is deducted.

### 70

Juan, though careless, young, and magnifique,
And rich in rubles, diamonds, cash, and credit,
Who did not limit much his bills per week,
Yet stared at this a little, though he paid it,–
(His Maggior Duomo, a smart, subtle Greek,
Before him summ'd the awful scroll and read it:)
But doubtless as the air, though seldom sunny,
Is free, the respiration's worth the money.

On with the horses! Off to Canterbury!
Tramp, tramp o'er pebble, and splash, splash
                       through puddle;
Hurrah! how swiftly speeds the post so merry!
Not like slow Germany, wherein they muddle
Along the road, as if they went to bury
Their fare; and also pause besides, to fuddle
With 'schnapps' – sad dogs! whom 'Hundsfot',
                       or 'Verflucter,'
Affect no more than lightning a conductor.

Now there is nothing gives a man such spirits,
Leavening his blood as cayenne doth a curry,
As going at full speed – no matter where its
Direction be, so 'tis but in a hurry,
And merely for the sake of its own merits:
For the less cause there is for all this flurry,
The greater is the pleasure in arriving
At the great *end* of travel – which is driving.

They saw at Canterbury the cathedral;
Black Edward's helm, and Becket's bloody stone,
Were pointed out as usual by the bedral,
In the same quaint, uninterested tone:–
There's glory again for all, gentle reader! All
Ends in a rusty casque and dubious bone,
Half-solved into those sodas or magnesias,
Which form that bitter draught, the human species.

The effect on Juan was of course sublime:
He breathed a thousand Cressys, as he saw
That casque, which never stoop'd except to Time.
Even the bold Churchman's tomb excited awe,
Who died in the then great attempt to climb
O'er kings, who *now* at least *must talk* of law
Before they butcher. Little Leila gazed,
And asked why such a structure had been raised:

And being told it was 'God's house,' she said
He was well lodged, but only wonder'd how
He suffer'd Infidels in his homestead,
The cruel Nazarenes, who had laid low
His holy temples in the lands which bred
The True Believers;– and her infant brow
Was bent with grief that Mahomet should resign
A mosque so noble, flung like pearls to swine.

On! on! through meadows, managed like a garden,
A paradise of hope and high production;
For after years of travel by a bard in
Countries of greater heat, but lesser suction,
A green field is a sight which makes him pardon
The absence of that more sublime construction!
Which mixes up vines, olives, precipices,
Glaciers, volcanos, oranges, and ices.

And when I think upon a pot of beer –
But I won't weep! – and so drive on, postilions!
As the smart boys spurr'd fast in their career,
Juan admired these highways of free millions;
A country in all senses the most dear
To foreigner or native, save some silly ones,
Who 'kick against the pricks' just at this juncture,
And for their pains get only a fresh puncture.

What a delightful thing's a turn-pike road!
So smooth, so level, such a mode of shaving
The earth, as scarce the eagle in the broad
Air can accomplish, with his wide wings waving.
Had such been cut in Phaeton's time, the god
Had told his son to satisfy his craving
With the York mail; – but onward as we roll,
'Surgit amari aliquid' – the toll!

LORD BYRON (1788–1824)

W. H. Auden lived much of his creative life in the United States and was a naturalised American citizen. In old age, he returned to England, however, as this tender Horatian celebration shows.

## Thank You, Fog

Grown used to New York weather,
all too familiar with Smog,
You, Her unsullied Sister,
I'd quite forgotten and what
You bring to British winters:
now native knowledge returns.

Sworn foe to festination,
daunter of drivers and planes,
volants, of course, will curse You,
but how delighted I am
that You've been lured to visit
Wiltshire's witching countryside
for a whole week at Christmas,
that no one can scurry where
my cosmos is contracted
to an ancient manor-house
and four Selves, joined in friendship,
Jimmy, Tania, Sonia, Me.

Outdoors a shapeless silence,
for even those birds whose blood
is brisk enough to bid them
abide here all the year round,
like the merle and the mavis
at Your cajoling refrain
their jocund interjections,

no cock considers a scream,
vaguely visible, tree-tops
rustle not but stay there, so
efficiently condensing
Your damp to definite drops.

Indoors specific spaces,
cosy, accommodate to
reminiscence and reading,
crosswords, affinities, fun:
refected by a sapid
supper and regaled by wine,
we sit in a glad circle,
each unaware of our own
nose but alert to the others,
making the most of it, for
how soon we must re-enter,
when lenient days are done,
the world of work and money
and minding our p's and q's.

No summer sun will ever
dismantle the global gloom
cast by the Daily Papers,
vomiting in slip-shod prose
the facts of filth and violence
that we're too dumb to prevent:
our earth's a sorry spot, but
for this special interim,
so restful yet so festive,
Thank you, Thank You, Thank You, Fog.

W. H. AUDEN (1907–73)

Windsor Forest is still one of the most beautiful places in England, but since the building of Heathrow Airport it can only be enjoyed by the deaf. Alexander Pope was brought up on the edge of Windsor Forest and began to write this account of its beauties in 1704, when he was sixteen. His physical deformities – he was a bony little dwarf – came upon him after an illness at the age of twelve. The joy of knowing that a Stuart was on the throne was particularly intense for the Popes who, appropriately given their surname, were Catholics: hence the fact that Alexander was educated at home, eschewing either a public school or attendance at a university (which would have required him to take a Protestant oath).

### FROM Windsor-Forest

Thy forests, Windsor! and thy green retreats,
At once the Monarch's and the Muse's seats,
Invite my lays. Be present, sylvan maids!
Unlock your springs, and open all your shades.
The Groves of Eden, vanish'd now so long,
Live in description, and look green in song:
These, were my breast inspir'd with equal flame,
Like them in beauty, should be like in fame.
Here waving groves a chequer'd scene display,
And part admit, and part exclude the day;
As some coy nymph her lover's warm address
Nor quite indulges, nor can quite repress.
There, interspers'd in laws and op'ning glades,
Thin trees arise that shun each other's shades.
Here in full light the russet plains extend:
There wrapt in clouds the blueish hills ascend.
Ev'n the wild heath displays her purple dyes,

43

And 'midst the desert fruitful fields arise,
That crown'd with tufted trees and springing corn,
Like verdant isles the sable waste adorn.
Not proud Olympus yields a nobler sight,
Tho' Gods assembled grace his tow'ring height,
Than what more humble mountains offer here,
Where, in their blessings, all those Gods appear.
See Pan with flocks, with fruits Pomona crown'd,
Here blushing Flora paints th'enamel'd ground,
Here Ceres' gifts in waving prospect stand,
And nodding tempt the joyful reaper's hand;
Rich Industry sits smiling on the plains,
And peace and plenty tell, a STUART reigns.

ALEXANDER POPE (1688–1744)

Robert Browning left England romantically: he rescued his wife
Elizabeth Barrett (six years his senior) from the tyranny of her
father, Mr Barrett of Wimpole Street. They married secretly in
1846 and lived very happily together in Florence until 1861. But,
as his most famous poem of exile showed, he missed England.


## Home-thoughts, from Abroad

O to be in England
Now that April's there,
And whoever wakes in England
Sees, some morning, unaware,
That the lowest boughs and the brushwood sheaf
Round the elm-tree bole are in tiny leaf,
While the chaffinch sings on the orchard bough
In England – now!

And after April, when May follows,
And the whitethroat builds, and all the swallows!
Hark, where my blossom'd pear-tree in the hedge
Leans to the field and scatters on the clover
Blossoms and dewdrops – at the bent spray's edge –
That's the wise thrush; he sings each song twice over,
Lest you should think he never could recapture
The first fine careless rapture!
And though the fields look rough with hoary dew,
All will be gay when noontide wakes anew
The buttercups, the little children's dower
– Far brighter than this gaudy melon-flower!

ROBERT BROWNING (1812–89)

It would be a strange celebration of 'Albion's beauties' which did not contain at least one poem about the loveliness of an English Garden. Andrew Marvell probably wrote this poem when he was the tutor to the daughter of Lord Fairfax at Nun Appleton in Yorkshire.

## The Garden

### 1

How vainly men themselves amaze
To win the Palm, the Oke, or Bayes;
And their uncessant Labours see
Crown'd from some single Herb or Tree,
Whose short and narrow verged Shade
Does prudently their Toyles upbraid;
While all Flowr's and all Trees do close
To weave the Garlands of repose.

### 2

Fair quiet, have I found thee here,
And Innocence they Sister dear!
Mistaken long, I sought you then
In busie Companies of Men.
Your sacred Plants, if here below,
Only among the Plants will grow.
Society is all but rude,
To this delicious Solitude.

### 3

No white nor red was ever seen
So am'rous as this lovely green.
Fond Lovers, cruel as their Flame,
Cut in these Trees their Mistress name.
Little, Alas, they know, or heed,
How far these Beauties Hers exceed!
Fair Trees! Where s'eer your barkes I wound,
No Name shall but your own be found.

### 4

When we have run our Passions heat,
Love hither makes his best retreat.
The *Gods*, that moral Beauty chase.
Still in a Tree did end their race.
*Apollo* hunted *Daphne* so,
Only that She might Laurel grow.
And *Pan* did after *Syrinx* speed,
Not as a Nymph, but for a Reed.

What wond'rous Life in this I lead!
Ripe Apples drop about my head;
The Luscious Clusters of the Vine
Upon my Mouth do crush their Wine;
The Nectaren, and curious Peach,
Into my hands themselves do reach;
Stumbling on Melons, as I pass,
Insnar'd with Flow'rs, I fall on Grass.

Meanwhile the Mind, from pleasure less,
Withdraws into its happiness:
The Mind, that Ocean where each kind
Does streight its own resemblance find;
Yet it creates, transcending these,
Far other Worlds, and other Seas;
Annihilating all that's made
To a green Thought in a green Shade.

Here at the Fountains sliding foot,
Or at some Fruit-trees mossy root,
Casting the Bodies Vest aside,
My Soul into the boughs does glide:
There like a Bird it sits, and sings,
Then whets, and combs its silver Wings;
And, till prepar'd for longer flight,
Waves in its Plumes the various Light.

### 8

Such was that happy Garden-state,
While Man there walk'd without a Mate:
After a Place so pure, and sweet,
What other Help could yet be meet!
But 'twas beyond a Mortal's share
To wander solitary there:
Two Paradises 'twere in one
To live in Paradise alone.

### 9

How well the skilful Gardner drew
Of flow'rs and herbes this Dial new;
Where from above the milder Sun
Does through a fragrant Zodiack run;
And, as its works, th' industrious Bee
Computes its time as well as we.
How could such sweet and wholsome Hours
Be reckon'd but with herbs and flow'rs!

ANDREW MARVELL (1621–78)

Geoffrey Hill grew up in the West Midlands, and he has an extraordinary gift for evoking the essence of place. His 'The Herefordshire Carol' is one of the poems which comes into my head when I think of England.

## The Herefordshire Carol

So to celebrate that kingdom: it grows
greener in winter, essence of the year;
the apple-branches musty with green fur.
In the viridian darkness of its yews

it is an enclave of perpetual vows
broken in time. Its truth shows disrepair,
disfigured shrines, their stones of gossamer,
Old Moore's astrology, all hallows,

the squire's effigy bewigged with frost,
and hobnails cracking puddles before dawn.
In grange and cottage girls rise from their beds

by candlelight and mend their ruined braids.
Touched by the cry of the iconoclast,
how the rose-window blossoms with the sun!

GEOFFREY HILL (1932– )

John Clare was a poor man of small education who spent much of his life in the Northampton lunatic asylum. His poems evoke the understated landscapes of his native county. 'Mist in the Meadows', written in the asylum, is typical.

## Mist in the Meadows

The even oer the meadow seems to stoop
More distant lessens the diminished spire
Mist in the hollows reaks and curdles up
Like fallen clouds that spread – and things retire
Less seen and less – the shepherd passes near
And little distant most grotesquely shades
As walking without legs – lost to his knees
As through the rawky creeping smoke he wades
Now half way up the arches disappear
And small the bits of sky that glimmer through
Then trees loose all but tops – I meet the fields
And now the indistinctness passes bye
The shepherd all his length is seen again
And further on the village meets the eye

JOHN CLARE (1793–1864)

Tennyson's verse photographs English landscape and seascape while suffusing it with his own emotions. *In Memoriam* was a long series of lyrics in which he tried to come to terms with personal grief at the loss of a close friend, Arthur Hallam, and with the religious doubts caused by scientific advance. In this lyric, on country walks in springtime, he longs for his friend's form to appear before him, as he catches sight of an early king-fisher: the sea-blue bird of March.

When rosy plumelets tuft the larch,
    And rarely pipes the mounted thrush;
    Or underneath the barren bush
Flits by the sea-blue bird of March;

Come, wear the form by which I know
    Thy spirit in time among thy peers;
    The hope of unaccomplish'd years
Be large and lucid round thy brow.

When summer's hourly-mellowing change
    May breathe, with many roses sweet,
    Upon the thousand waves of wheat,
That ripple round the lonely grange;

Come: not in watches of the night,
    But where the sunbeam broodeth warm,
    Come, beauteous in thine after form,
And like a finer light in light.

ALFRED, LORD TENNYSON (1809–92)

The English beauties with whom Algernon Charles Swinburne is often associated are the prostitutes of St John's Wood, whom he liked to visit during his dissipated youth.

> Cold eyelids that hide like a jewel
>   Hard eyes that grow soft for an hour;
> The heavy white limbs, and the cruel
>   Red mouth like a venomous flower;
> When these are gone by with their glories,
>   What shall rest of thee then, what remain,
> O mystic and sombre Dolores,
>   Our Lady of Pain?

*from* 'Dolores (Notre-Dame des Sept Douleurs)'
A. C. SWINBURNE (1837–1909)

But like his master Baudelaire, Swinburne was a great nature poet. Not only Bonchurch on the Isle of Wight, where he grew up, but also Northumberland, the home of his ancestors, inspired him. Swinburne was a prolix poet which partly explains his unread status in our impatient age, but, as these stanzas extracted from 'Winter in Northumberland' show, he was a lyricist of almost unmatched art.

## FROM Winter in Northumberland

### I

Outside the garden
The wet skies harden;
The gates are barred on
   The summer side:
'Shut out the flower-time,
Sunbeam and shower-time;
Make way for our time,'
   Wild winds have cried.
Green once and cheery,
The woods, worn weary,
Sigh as the dreary
   Weak sun goes home:
A great wind grapples
The wave, and dapples
The dead green floor of the sea with foam.

Through fell and moorland,
And salt-sea foreland,
Our noisy norland
   Resounds and rings;

Waste waves thereunder
Are blown in sunder,
And winds make thunder
    With cloudwide wings;
Sea-drift makes dimmer
The beacon's glimmer;
Nor sail nor swimmer
    Can try the tides;
And snowdrifts thicken
Where, when leaves quicken,
Under the heather the sundew hides.

Green land and red land,
Moorside and headland,
Are white as dead land,
    Are all as one;
Nor honied heather,
Nor bells to gather,
Fair with fair weather
    And faithful sun:
Fierce frost has eaten
All flowers that sweeten
The fells rain-beaten;
    And winds their foes
Have made the snow's bed
Down in the rose-bed;
Deep in the snow's bed bury the rose.

In fierce March weather
White waves break tether,
And whirled together
    At either hand,

Like weeds uplifted,
The tree-trunks rifted
In spars are drifted,
   Like foam or sand,
Past swamp and sallow
And reed-beds callow,
Through pool and shallow,
   To wind and lee,
Till, no more tongue-tied,
Full flood and young tide
Roar down the rapids and storm the sea.

O stout north-easter,
Sea-king, land-waster,
For all thine haste, or
   Thy stormy skill,
Yet hadst thou never,
For all endeavour,
Strength to dissever
   Or strength to spill,
Save of his giving
Who gave our living,
Whose hands are weaving
   What ours fulfil;
Whose feet tread under
The storms and thunder,
Who made our wonder to work his will.

A. C. SWINBURNE (1837–1909)

Speaking personally, I would not have wanted to live before the invention of the bicycle. The pleasure of whizzing along is unlike any other. Perhaps the first poet to immortalise the joy of the bike was Henry Charles Beeching. He was a clergyman who became Dean of Norwich. A Balliol man, he made up the verses about Benjamin Jowett, the translator of Pluto and Master of Balliol who transformed Oxford – and hence the whole of British higher education.

> First come I: my name is Jowett
> There's no knowledge but I know it.
> I am the Master of this College,
> What I don't know isn't knowledge.

But here is Beeching on the pleasure of free-wheeling. Very English, not least because it was in the Gloucestershire village of Dursley that the Danish engineer Mikael Pedersen pioneered the first lightweight modern bike, the Dursley-Pedersen.

## Going down Hill on a Bicycle

*A Boy's Song*

> With lifted feet, hands still,
> I am poised, and down the hill
> Dart, with heedful mind;
> The air goes by in a wind.
>
> Swifter and yet more swift,
> Till the heart with a mighty lift
> Makes the lungs laugh, the throat cry:–
> 'O bird, see; see, bird, I fly!

'Is this, is this your joy?
O bird, then I, though a boy,
For a golden moment share
Your feathery life in air!'

Say, heart, is there aught like this
In a world that is full of bliss?
'Tis more than skating, bound
Steel-shod to the level ground.

Speed slackens now, I float
Awhile in my airy boat;
Till, when the wheels scarce crawl,
My feet to the treadles fall.

Alas, that the longest hill
Must end in a vale; but still,
Who climbs with toil, wheresoe'er,
Shall find wings waiting there.

HENRY CHARLES BEECHING (1859–1919)

John Davidson was a Scotsman but he met his tragic end, drowning himself, at Penzance. He was a fine playwright and poet. His verses about Romney Marsh come close, as a poem may, to a landscape painting.

## In Romney Marsh

As I went down to Dymchurch Wall,
　　I heard the South sing o'er the land;
I saw the yellow sunlight fall
　　On knolls where Norman churches stand.

And ringing shrilly, taut and lithe,
　　Within the wind a core of sound,
The wire from Romney town to Hythe
　　Alone its airy journey wound.

A veil of purple vapour flowed
　　And trail'd its fringe along the Straits;
The upper air like sapphire glow'd;
　　And roses fill'd Heaven's central gates.

Masts in the offing wagg'd their tops;
　　The swinging waves peal'd on the shore;
The saffron beach, all diamond drops
　　And beads of surge, prolong'd the roar.

As I came up from Dymchurch Wall,
　　I saw above the Downs' low crest
The crimson brands of sunset fall,
　　Flicker and fade from out the west.

Night sank: like flakes of silver fire
    The stars in one great shower came down;
Shrill blew the wind; and shrill the wire
    Rang out from Hythe to Romney town.

The darkly shining salt sea drops
    Streamed as the waves clashed on the shore;
The beach, with all its organ stops
    Pealing again, prolong'd the roar.

JOHN DAVIDSON (1857–1909)

William Barnes's long life was spent in Dorset. First he worked as a solicitor's clerk, then as a teacher. Finally, he took Holy Orders. When he died in 1886, his obituary in *The Saturday Review* said, 'There is no doubt that he is the best pastoral poet we possess, the most sincere, the most genuine, the most theocritan; and that the dialect is but a very thin veil hiding from us some of the most delicate and finished verse written in our time.'

## Leaves a-Vallen

There the ash-tree leaves do vall
    In the wind a-blowen cwolder,
An' my children, tall or small,
    Since last Fall be woone year wolder;
Woone year wolder, woone year dearer,
    Till when they do leave my he'th.
I shall be noo mwore a hearer
    O' their vaices or their me'th.

There dead ash leaves be a-toss'd
  In the wind, a-blowen stronger,
An' our life-time, since we lost
  Souls we lov'd, is woone year longer;
Woone year longer, woone year wider,
  Vrom the friends that death ha' took,
As the hours do teake the rider
  Vrom the hand that last he shook.

No. If he do ride at night
  Vrom the zide the zun went under,
Woone hour vrom his western light
  Needen meake woone hour asunder;
Woone hour onward, woone hour nigher
  To the hopevul eastern skies,
Where his mornen rim o'vier
  Soon agean shall meet his eyes.

Leaves be now a-scatter'd round
  In the wind, a blowen bleaker,
An' if we do walk the ground
  Wi' our life-strangth woone year weaker;
Woone year weaker, woone year nigher
  To the pleace where we shall vind
Woone that's deathless vor the dier,
  Voremost they that dropp'd behind.

WILLIAM BARNES (1801–86)

And, of course, there is the pleasure of social life. W. M. Praed's 'society verses' evoke the world of the Regency in which he flourished during his short life. (He was not quite thirty-seven when he died in 1839.) The characters have changed – not many Bishops at grand London parties these days – but some things – 'The ice of her Ladyship's manners' – do not change.

## Good Night to the Season

Good night to the Season! 'Tis over!
    Gay dwellings no longer are gay;
The courtier, the gambler, the lover,
    Are scattered like swallows away:
There's nobody left to invite one
    Except my good uncle and spouse;
My mistress is bathing at Brighton,
    My patron is sailing at Cowes:
For want of a better employment,
    Till Ponto and Don can get out,
I'll cultivate rural enjoyment,
    And angle immensely for trout.

Good night to the Season! – the lobbies,
    Their changes, and rumours of change,
Which startled the rustic Sir Bobbies,
    And made all the Bishops look strange;
The breaches, and battles, and blunders,
    Performed by the Commons and Peers;
The Marquis's eloquent blunders,
    The Baronet's eloquent ears;
Denouncings of Papists and treasons,
    Of foreign dominion and oats;

Misrepresentations of reasons,
　　And misunderstandings of notes.

Good night to the Season! – the buildings
　　Enough to make Inigo sick;
The paintings, and plasterings, and gildings
　　Of stucco, and marble, and brick;
The orders deliciously blended,
　　From love of effect, into one;
The club-houses only intended,
　　The palaces only begun;
The hell, where the fiend in his glory
　　Sits staring at putty and stones,
And scrambles from story to story,
　　To rattle at midnight his bones.

Good night to the Season! – the dances,
　　The fillings of hot little rooms,
The glancings of rapturous glances,
　　The fancyings of fancy costumes;
The pleasures which fashion makes duties,
　　The praisings of fiddles and flutes,
The luxury of looking at Beauties,
　　The tedium of talking to mutes;
The female diplomatists, planners
　　Of matches for Laura and Jane;
The ice of her Ladyship's manners,
　　The ice of his Lordship's champagne.

Good night to the Season! – the rages
　　Led off by the chiefs of the throng,
The Lady Matilda's new pages,
　　The Lady Eliza's new song;
Miss Fennel's macaw, which at Boodle's

Was held to have something to say;
Mrs. Splenetic's musical poodles,
    Which bark '*Batti Batti*' all day;
The pony Sir Araby sported,
    As hot and as black as a coal,
And the Lion his mother imported,
    In bearskins and grease, from the Pole.

Good night to the Season! – the Toso,
    So very majestic and tall;
Miss Ayton, whose singing was so-so,
    And Pasta, divinest of all;
The labour in vain of the ballet,
    So sadly deficient in stars;
The foreigners thronging the Alley,
    Exhaling the breath of cigars;
The *loge* where some heiress (how killing!)
    Environed with exquisites sits,
The lovely one out of her drilling,
    The silly ones out of their wits.

Good night to the Season! – the splendour
    That beamed in the Spanish Bazaar;
Where I purchased – my heart was so tender –
    A card-case, a pasteboard guitar,
A bottle of perfume, a girdle,
    A lithographed Riego, full-grown,
Whom bigotry drew on a hurdle
    That artists might draw him on stone;
A small panorama of Seville,
    A trap for demolishing flies,
A caricature of the Devil,
    And a look from Miss Sheridan's eyes.

Good night to the Season! – the flowers
   Of the grand horticultural fete,
When boudoirs were quitted for bowers,
   And the fashion was – not to be late;
When all who had money and leisure
   Grew rural o'er ices and wines,
All pleasantly toiling for pleasure,
   All hungrily pining for pines,
And making of beautiful speeches,
   And marring of beautiful shows,
And feeding on delicate peaches,
   And treading on delicate toes.

Good night to the Season! – Another
   Will come, with its trifles and toys,
And hurry away, like its brother,
   In sunshine, and odour, and noise.
Will it come with a rose or a briar?
   Will it come with a blessing or curse?
Will its bonnets be lower or higher?
   Will its morals be better or worse?
Will it find me grown thinner or fatter,
   Or fonder or wrong or of right,
Or married – or buried? – no matter:
   Good night to the Season – good night!

W. M. PRAED (1802–39)

Felicia Hemans is best remembered today for two poems – 'Casabianca', whose opening line is 'The boy stood on the burning deck' – and 'The Homes of England'. Noel Coward took up her first stanza and made it into an amusing song about the stately homes of England in their decline. But Felicia celebrated not merely the stately, but also the cottage, homes.

## The Homes of England

The stately Homes of England,
  How beautiful they stand!
Amidst their tall ancestral trees,
  O'er all the pleasant land.
The deer across their greensward bound
  Through shade and sunny gleam,
And the swan glides past them with the sound
  Of some rejoicing stream.

The merry Homes of England!
  Around their hearths by night,
What gladsome looks of household love
  Meet in the ruddy light!
There woman's voice flows forth in song,
  Or childish tale is told;
Or lips move tunefully along
  Some glorious page of old.

The blessed Homes of England!
  How softly on their bowers
Is laid the holy quietness
  That breathes from Sabbath hours!

Solemn, yet sweet, the church bell's chime
  Floats through their woods at morn;
All other sounds, in that still time,
  Of breeze and leaf are born.

The cottage Homes of England!
  By thousands on her plains,
They are smiling o'er the silvery brooks,
  And round the hamlet-fanes.
Through glowing orchards forth they peep,
  Each from its nook of leaves;
And fearless there the lowly sleep,
  As the bird beneath their eaves.

The free fair Homes of England!
  Long, long in hut and hall,
May hearts of native proof be reared
  To guard each hallow'd wall!
And green for ever be the groves,
  And bright the flowery sod,
Where first the child's glad spirit loves
  Its country and its God!

FELICIA HEMANS (1793–1835)

66

As a non-doggy person I feel obliged to admit that England is a very doggy place. Stevie Smith celebrates the fact in this short, characteristic poem.

## O Happy Dogs of England

O happy dogs of England
Bark well as well you may
If you lived anywhere else
You would not be so gay.

O happy dogs of England
Bark well at errand boys
If you lived anywhere else
You would not be allowed to make
        such an infernal noise.

STEVIE SMITH (1902–71)

# FIVE

# PLATONIC ENGLAND

Geoffrey Hill evokes 'Platonic England', borrowing the phrase from Samuel Taylor Coleridge. In this section, I have gathered together poems and one, once familiar, prayer, which evoke this Ideal Place, this England of the mind.

## A Jacobite's Epitaph

To my true king I offered free from stain
Courage and faith; vain faith, and courage vain.
For him I threw lands, honours, wealth, away,
And one dear hope, that was more prized than they.
For him I languished in a foreign clime,
Grey-haired with sorrow in my manhood's prime;
Heard on Lavernia Scargill's whispering trees,
And pined by Arno for my lovelier Tees;
Beheld each night my home in fevered sleep,
Each morning started from the dream to weep;
Till God, who saw me tried too sorely, gave
The resting-place I asked, an early grave.
O thou, whom chance leads to this nameless stone,
From that proud country which was once mine own,
By those white cliffs I never more must see,
By that dear language which I spake like thee,
Forget all feuds, and shed one English tear
O'er English dust. A broken heart lies here.

THOMAS BABINGTON MACAULAY (1800–59)

## from A Lincolnshire Church

Greyly tremendous the thunder
Hung over the width of the wold
But here the green marsh was alight
In a huge cloud cavern of gold,
And there, on a gentle eminence,
Topping some ash trees, a tower
Silver and brown in the sunlight,
Worn by sea-wind and shower,
Lincolnshire Middle Pointed.
And around it, turning their backs,
The usual sprinkle of villas;
The usual woman in slacks,
Cigarette in her mouth,
Regretting Americans, stands
As a wireless croons in the kitchen
Manicuring her hands.
Dear old, bloody old England
Of telegraph poles and tin,
Seemingly so indifferent
And with so little soul to win . . .

JOHN BETJEMAN (1906–84)


33

On forelands high in heaven,
  'Tis many a year gone by,
Amidst the fall of even
  Would stand my friends and I.
Before our foolish faces

Lay lands we did not see;
Our eyes were in the places
    Where we should never be.

'Oh, the pearl seas are yonder,
    The amber-sanded shore;
Shires where the girls are fonder,
    Towns where the pots hold more.
And here fret we and moulder
    By grange and rick and shed
And every moon are older,
    And soon we shall be dead.'

Heigho, 'twas true and pity;
    But there we lads must stay.
Troy was a steepled city,
    But Troy was far away.
And round we turned lamenting
    To homes we longed to leave,
And silent hills indenting
    The orange band of eve.

I see the air benighted
    And all the dusking dales,
And lamps in England lighted,
    And evening wrecked on Wales;
And starry darkness paces
    The road from sea to sea,
And blots the foolish faces
    Of my poor friends and me.

                    A. E. HOUSMAN (1859–1936)

# Jerusalem

And did those feet in ancient time
Walk upon England's mountains green?
And was the holy Lamb of God
On England pleasant pastures seen?

And did the Countenance Divine
Shine forth upon our clouded hills?
And was Jerusalem builded here
Among these dark Satanic Mills?

Brine me my Bow of burning gold!
Bring me my Arrows of desire!
Bring me my Spear! O clouds, unfold!
Bring me my Chariot of fire!

I will not cease from Mental Fight,
Nor shall my Sword sleep in my hand,
Till we have built Jerusalem
In England's green and pleasant land.

WILLIAM BLAKE (1757–1827)

The Housman, the extract from Betjeman and Blake's 'Jerusalem'
– they found their way here on their own. But are we right to
include Matthew Arnold's 'Dover Beach', first published in 1867?
It is a fine poem – but is it evoking something essentially English?
I believe so. Arnold belonged to that great Victorian generation
who had to live with religious doubt. Indeed, it could be said
that they invented it. The heyday of the British Empire, of British

political power, was also the time of the greatest intellectual torment – scientific research and biblical scholarship destroying the faith of many thinking people. Matthew Arnold's father Thomas was the headmaster of Rugby School. The father was a robust Broad Churchman (not an evangelical as is sometimes said) but he was not troubled, fundamentally, by doubt. Matthew Arnold was. He wondered whether there was any future in Christianity itself. As a schools inspector, who faithfully journeyed around England visiting the schools attended by the poor, he knew it better than most, and had cause to meditate on what Betjeman called 'bloody old England'. It is one of the finest poems in our language. And yes, the doubt in the withdrawing roar of the shingle *is* very English.


## Dover Beach

The sea is calm to-night,
The tide is full, the moon lies fair
Upon the Straits; – on the French coast, the light
Gleams, and is gone; the cliffs of England stand,
Glimmering and vast, out in the tranquil bay.
Come to the window, sweet is the night air!
Only, from the long line of spray
Where the ebb meets the moon-blanch'd sand,
Listen! You hear the grating roar
Of pebbles which the waves suck back, and fling,
At their return, up the high strand,
Begin, and cease, and then again begin,
With tremulous cadence slow, and bring
The eternal note of sadness in.

Sophocles long ago
Heard it on the Aegaean, and it brought
Into his mind the turbid ebb and flow
Of human misery; we
Find also in the sound a thought,
Hearing it by this distant northern sea.

The sea of faith
Was once, too, at the full, and round earth's shore
Lay like the folds of a bright girdle furl'd;
But now I only hear
Its melancholy, long, withdrawing roar,
Retreating to the breath
Of the night-wind down the vast edges drear
And naked shingles of the world.

Ah, love, let us be true
To one another! for the world, which seems
To lie before us like a land of dreams,
So various, so beautiful, so new,
Hath really neither joy, nor love, nor light,
Nor certitude, nor peace, nor help for pain;
And we are here as on a darkling plain
Swept with confused alarms of struggle and flight,
Where ignorant armies clash by night.

MATTHEW ARNOLD (1822–88)

W. S. Gilbert sounds a coarser note, but the song is a good one. In Alan Bennett's televised play about the Communist spy Guy Burgess, this Gilbert and Sullivan number blares out as the archetypical Englishman, with his suits made by a London tailor and his shoes from St James's Street, marches across the bleak streets of Soviet Moscow. Bennett beautifully captures the tragic irony of a man who is conservative in everything but politics.

### FROM *HMS Pinafore*

Ralph and Jos (I, He) humble, poor, and lowly born,
　　The meanest in the port division –
　　The butt of epauletted scorn –
　　The mark of quarter-deck derision –
(Have, Has) dared to raise (my, his) wormy eyes
　　Above the dust to which you'd mould (me, him)
　　　　In manhood's glorious pride to rise,
　　(I am, He is) an Englishman – behold (me! him!)

*All*　He is an Englishman!

*Boat*　He is an Englishman!
　　　　For he himself has said it,
　　　　And it's greatly to his credit,
　　That he is an Englishman!

*All*　That he is an Englishman!

*Boat*　For he might have been a Roosian,
　　　　A French, or Turk, or Proosian,
　　　　Or perhaps Itali–an!

75

| *All* | Or perhaps Itali–an! |

| *Boat* | But in spite of all temptations |
| | To belong to other nations, |
| | He remains an Englishman! |

| *All* | For in spite of all temptations, etc. |

W. S. GILBERT (1836–1911)

Should anyone doubt my contention that 'England is no more', I should challenge her, or him, to read aloud this prayer at a gathering of contemporary parliamentarians. There must always have been an ironic contrast between the sublime words written by Thomas Cranmer and the actual reality of what Members of Parliament were like. But until comparatively recently, this prayer 'For the High Court of Parliament' reflected an England which did actually exist. Now, it is not just that the words are 'old fashioned'. The England summoned up by the prayer – so euphonious as to be in reality a sort of poem – is one which we can all see has departed.


## A Prayer for the High Court of Parliament, to be read during their Session

Most gracious God, we humbly beseech thee, as for this Kingdom in general, so especially for the High Court in Parliament, under our most religious and gracious Queen at this time assembled: That thou wouldest be pleased to direct and prosper all their consultations to the advancement of thy glory, the good of thy Church, the safety, honour, and welfare of our Sovereign and her Dominions; that all things may be so ordered and settled by their endeavours, upon the best and surest foundations, that peace and happiness, truth and justice, religion and piety, may be established among us for all generations. These and all other necessaries, for them, for us, and thy whole Church, we humbly beg in the Name and Mediation of Jesus Christ our most blessed Lord and Saviour. *Amen.*

THOMAS CRANMER (1489–1556)

When George V died in 1936 – the same year as Kipling – many must have felt that they had lost something more than just a countrified, peppery old constitutional monarch. He stood for something, if ever an English king has done. And that something was to be swept away by the advent of the modern, and by the war. This feeling of what the late King stood for is encapsulated in Betjeman's beautifully understated poem.

## Death of King George V

'New King arrives in his capital by air . . . ' *Daily Newspaper*

Spirits of well-shot woodcock, partridge, snipe
    Flutter and bear him up the Norfolk sky:
In that red house in a red mahogany book-case
    The stamp collection waits with mounts long dry.

The big blue eyes are shut which saw wrong clothing
    And favourite fields and coverts from a horse;
Old men in country houses hear clocks ticking
    Over thick carpets with a deadened force;

Old men who never cheated, never doubted,
   Communicated monthly, sit and stare
At the new suburb stretched beyond the run-way
   Where a young man lands hatless from the air.

JOHN BETJEMAN (1906–84)

# SIX

# WRECKAGE

This section is not simply about architectural wreckage. And, as the first poem shows, the belief that England is down the drain has been around for a long time. William Wordsworth wrote his sonnet calling up the spirit of John Milton before his conversion to Toryism. Had Milton visited the England of 1802, he would probably have hated it, but he would at least have recognised it as England. Whereas if he came back today, he would find a country in which he was a stranger.

Much of this is attributable to the physical wreckage of England. Betjeman, in his anger at the farmers spraying England's crops with poison, was a prophet who wrote a whole generation before the Green movement. In his war on the spivs who pulled down so many English town centres and replaced them with brutalist lumps – solely for money – he sometimes seemed to be alone. Only when we stood among the wreckage did we realise how right he had been in his campaigns against the criminals who destroyed England. Philip Larkin describes the same process in his bleak realistic poem 'Going, Going'.

I have ended the section, however, with a poem from an earlier era. Hilaire Belloc's humorous verses were written when – physically speaking – England was all in one piece. But the selfishness of English society, which so disgusted the young Wordsworth, had reached an apogee in Hilaire Belloc's Edwardian England. During the Second World War, supposedly England's finest hour, class differences were laid aside. But at the beginning of the twenty-first century, the 'hoary social curse gets hoarier and hoarier.' As all the poets here assembled would agree, the cure for such selfishness is not to be found in politics. For Larkin, the answer was despair and drink. For others, it was religion.

### FROM England 1802

Milton! Thou shouldst be living at this hour:
   England hath need of thee: she is a fen
   Of stagnant waters: altar, sword, and pen,
Fireside, the heroic wealth of hall and bower,
Have forfeited their ancient English dower
   Of inward happiness. We are selfish men;
   O raise us up, return to us again,
And give us manners, virtue, freedom, power!
Thy soul was like a Star, and dwelt apart;
   Thou hadst a voice whose sound was like the sea:
   Pure as the naked heavens, majestic, free,
   So didst thou travel on life's common way,
In cheerful godliness; and yet thy heart
   The lowliest duties on herself did lay.

WILLIAM WORDSWORTH (1770–1850)

# Executive

I am a young executive. No cuffs than mine are cleaner;
I have a Slimline brief-case and I use the firm's Cortina.
In every roadside hostelry from here to Burgess Hill
The *maître d'hôtel* all know me well and let me sign the bill.

You ask me what it is I do. Well actually, you know,
I'm partly a liaison man and partly P.R.O.
Essentially I integrate the current export drive
And basically I'm viable from ten o'clock till five.

For vital off-the-record work – that's talking transport-wise –
I've a scarlet Aston-Martin – and does she go? She flies!
Pedestrians and dogs and cats – we mark them down for slaughter.
I also own a speed-boat which has never touched the water.

She's built of fibre-glass, of course. I call her 'Mandy Jane'
After a bird I used to know – No soda, please, just plain –
And how did I acquire her? Well to tell you about that
And to put you in the picture I must wear my other hat.

I do some mild developing. The sort of place I need
Is a quiet country market town that's rather run to seed.
A luncheon and a drink or two, a little *savoir faire* –
I fix the Planning Officer, the Town Clerk and the Mayor.

And if some preservationist attempts to interfere
A 'dangerous structure' notice from the Borough Engineer
Will settle any buildings that are standing in our way –
The modern style, sir, with respect, has really come to stay.

JOHN BETJEMAN (1906–84)

# Harvest Hymn

We spray the fields and scatter
  The poison on the ground
So that no wicked wild flowers
  Upon our farm be found.
We like whatever helps us
  To line our purse with pence;
The twenty-four-hour broiler-house
  And neat electric fence.

All concrete sheds around us
  And Jaguars in the yard,
The telly lounge and deep-freeze
  Are ours from working hard.

We fire the fields for harvest,
  The hedges swell the flame,
The oak trees and the cottages
  From which our fathers came.
We give no compensation
  The earth is ours today,
And if we lose on arable,
  Then bungalows will pay.

  All concrete sheds . . . etc.

JOHN BETJEMAN (1906–84)

# Going, Going

I thought it would last my time –
The sense that, beyond the town,
There would always be fields and farms,
Where the village louts could climb
Such trees as were not cut down;
I knew there'd be false alarms

In the papers about old streets
And split-level shopping, but some
Have always been left so far;
And when the old part retreats
As the bleak high-risers come
We can always escape in the car.

Things are tougher than we are, just
As earth will always respond
However we mess it about;
Chuck filth in the sea, if you must:
The tides will be clean beyond.
– But what do I feel now? Doubt?

Or age, simply? The crowd
Is young in the M1 café;
Their kids are screaming for more –
More houses, more parking allowed,
More caravan sites, more pay.
On the Business Page, a score

Of spectacled grins approve
Some takeover bid that entails
Five per cent profit (and ten

Per cent more in the estuaries): move
Your works to the unspoilt dales
(Grey area grants)! And when

You try to get near the sea
In the summer . . .
It seems, just now,
To be happening so very fast;
Despite all the land left free
For the first time I feel somehow
That it isn't going to last,

That before I snuff it, the whole
Boiling will be bricked in
Except for the tourist parts –
First slum of Europe: a role
It won't be so hard to win,
With a cast of crooks and tarts.

And that will be England gone,
The shadows, the meadows, the lanes,
The guildhalls, the carved choirs.
There'll be books; it will linger on
In galleries; but all that remains
For us will be concrete and tyres.

Most things are never meant.
This won't be, most likely: but greeds
And garbage are too thick-strewn
To be swept up now, or invent
Excuses that make them all needs.
I just think it will happen, soon.

PHILIP LARKIN (1922–85)

# The Garden Party

The Rich arrived in pairs
And also in Rolls Royces;
They talked of their affairs
In loud and strident voices.

(The Husbands and the Wives
Of this elect society
Lead independent lives
Of infinite variety.)

The Poor arrived in Fords,
Whose features they resembled,
They laughed to see so many Lords
And Ladies all assembled.

The People in Between
Looked underdone and harassed,
And out of place and mean
And horribly embarrassed.

For the hoary social curse
Gets hoarier and hoarier,
And it stinks a trifle worse
*Than in*
The Days of Queen Victoria,

*when*

*They married and gave in marriage,*
*They danced at the County Ball,*
*And some of them kept a carriage.*
AND THE FLOOD DESTROYED THEM ALL.

HILAIRE BELLOC (1870–1953)

# SEVEN

# THE INTERSECTION OF THE TIMELESS MOMENT

T. S. Eliot in 'Little Gidding', a place where Nicholas Ferrar and his family led a life of secluded prayer in the seventeenth century, focussed on timelessness which is rooted in place. 'England' is a concept. Individual landscapes, towns, villages, are concentrations of experience. It is these which live.

> . . . If you came this way,
> Taking any route, starting from anywhere,
> At any time or at any season,
> It would always be the same: you would have to put off
> Sense and notion. You are not here to verify,
> Instruct yourself, or inform curiosity
> Or carry report. You are here to kneel
> Where prayer has been valid. And prayer is more
> Than an order of words, the conscious occupation
> Of the praying mind, or the sound of the voice praying.
> And what the dead had no speech for, when living,
> They can tell you, being dead: the communication
> Of the dead is tongued with fire beyond the language of the living.
> Here, the intersection of the timeless moment
> Is England and nowhere. Never and always.

T. S. ELIOT (1888–1965)

John Meade Falkner, antiquary and armaments manufacturer, was the author of three immortal novels and he was also an accomplished versifier who heard the voice of the past – especially in church. (He was librarian at Durham Cathedral.) But this poem reflects his reaction to the remains of the Roman Villa at Chedworth.

## A Roman Villa

(Chedworth)

One evening when his ferret strayed
　　The keeper turned about,
And fetched a lantern and a spade
　　To dig the truant out.

Dark weeks the autumn sunset wore,
　　Wild winds were in the wood;
The black leaves of the sycamore
　　Lay trampled in the mud.

It seemed as though the Earth were sad,
　　That she must show again
Those ancient mysteries she had
　　Concealed from common men.

The woodman dug, and paused awhile
　　To hear the owlets call,
And then his mattock struck a tile,
　　And then a buried wall.

And so we stand to-day and trace
　　The Roman's lost abode,
And feel the sun that browned his face,
　　And tread the stones he trod.

Here where the shelving valley fills
  The streams of reedy Leach,
Where this green theatre of hills
  Is clothed with rustling beech,

He made his home and saw the sun
  Turn westward day by day,
And marked the changing seasons run
  From blossom to decay . . .

. . . Old Roman, in these woodland dells
  By Leach's reedy flow,
Amid the snow-white lily bells
  You planted long ago,

We wonder who you were, and now
  If still your memory clings
To this fair home on Cotswold's brow,
  To these sweet earthly things:

Or do your bones forgetful sleep
  In some forgotten tomb,
With all those other bones that keep
  The same oblivious gloom –

The Saxon with the battle-shout
  And ruin in his train,
The Dane who drove the Saxon out,
  The Frank who slew the Dane?

What though the gloom wait us and those
  That shall be yet to come,
Till every song at evening close
  And singers all are dumb, –

Thou and thy works shall never die,
    But still from age to age
Are with us everlastingly,
    A deathless heritage.

J. M. Falkner (1858–1932)

'England' is not merely landscape. It is also towns – as the remaining poems in this section attest. Louis MacNeice was at school (Marlborough) with Betjeman and subsequently taught classics at Birmingham University.

## Birmingham

Smoke from the train-gulf hid by hoardings blunders
    upward, the brakes of cars
Pipe as the policeman pivoting round raises his flat hand,
    bars
With his figure of a monolith Pharaoh the queue of fidgety
    machines
(Chromium dogs on the bonnet, faces behind the triplex
    screens),
Behind him the streets run away between the proud glass
    of shops,
Cubical scent-bottles artificial legs arctic foxes and electric
    mops,
But beyond this centre the slumward vista thins like a
    diagram:
There, unvisited, are Vulcan's forges who doesn't care a
    tinker's damn.

Splayed outwards through the suburbs' houses, houses for
      rest
Seducingly rigged by the builder, half-timbered houses with
        lips pressed
So tightly and eyes staring at the traffic through bleary haws
And only a six-inch grip of the racing earth in their
        concrete claws;
In these houses men as in a dream pursue the Platonic Forms
With wireless and cairn terriers and gadgets approximating
        to the fickle norms
And endeavour to find God and score one over the neighbour
By climbing tentatively upward on jerry-built beauty and
        sweated labour.

The lunch hour: the shops empty, shopgirls' faces relax
Diaphanous as green glass, empty as old almanacs
As incoherent with ticketed gewgaws tiered behind their
        heads
As the Burne-Jones windows in St Philip's broken by
        crawling leads;
Insipid colour, patches of emotion, Saturday thrills
(This theatre is sprayed with 'June') – the gutter take our
        old playbills,
Next week-end it is likely in the heart's funfair we shall pull
Strong enough on the handle to get back our money; or at
        any rate it is possible.

On shining lines the trams like vast sarcophagi move
Into the sky, plum after sunset, merging to duck's egg,
        barred with mauve
Zeppelin clouds, and Pentecost-like the cars' headlights
        bud

Out from sideroads and the traffic signals, crème-de-
     menthe or bull's blood,
Tell one to stop, the engine gently breathing, or to go on
To where like black pipes of organs in the frayed and fading
     zone
Of the West the factory chimneys on sullen sentry will all
     night wait
To call, in the harsh morning, sleep-stupid faces through
     the daily gate.

LOUIS MACNEICE (1907–63)

For me, England is a universe of which Oxford is the centre. I
include therefore two poems inspired by the place, the first by
Auden, the second by the 1890s poet Lionel Johnson – who
was an even heavier drinker than Auden himself; quite an
achievement.

## Oxford

Nature invades: old rooks in each college garden
Still talk, like agile babies, the language of feeling,
By towers a river still runs coastward and will run,
     Stones in those towers are utterly
     Satisfied still with their weight.

Mineral and creature, so deeply in love with themselves
Their sin of accidie excludes all others,
Challenge our high-strung students with a careless beauty,
     Setting a single error
     Against their countless faults.

Outside, some factories, then a whole green county
Where a cigarette comforts the evil, a hymn the weak,
Where thousands fidget and poke and spend their money:
    Eros Paidagogos
    Weeps on his virginal bed.

And over this talkative city like any other
Weep the non-attached angels. Here too the knowledge
                                                    of death
Is a consuming love, and the natural heart refuses
    A low unflattering voice
    That sleeps not till it find a hearing.

W. H. AUDEN (1907–73)


## Oxford

Over the four long years! And now there rings
One voice of freedom and regret: *Farewell!*
Now old remembrance sorrows, and now sings:
But song from sorrow, now, I cannot tell.

City of weather'd cloister and worn court;
Grey city of strong towers and clustering spires;
Where art's fresh loveliness would first resort;
Where lingering art kindled her latest fires! . . .

There Shelley dream'd his white Platonic dreams;
There, classic Landor throve on Roman thought;
There, Addison pursued his quiet themes;
There, smiled Erasmus, and there, Colet taught.

And there, O memory more sweet than all!
Lived he, whose eyes keep yet our passing light;
Whose crystal lips Athenian speech recall;
Who wears Rome's purple with least pride, most right.

That is the Oxford strong to charm us yet:
Eternal in her beauty and her past.
What, though her soul be vex'd? She can forget
Cares of an hour: only the great things last.

Only the gracious air, only the charm,
And ancient might of true humanities,
These nor assault of man, nor time, can harm:
Not these, nor Oxford with her memories.

Together have we walk'd with willing feet
Gardens of plenteous trees, bowering soft lawn;
Hills wither Arnold wander'd; and all sweet
June meadows, from the troubling world withdrawn;

Chapels of cedarn fragrance, and rich gloom
Pour'd from empurpled panes on either hand;
Cool pavements, carved with legends of the tomb;
Grave haunts, where we might dream, and understand . . .

All times may be; she hath no thought of time:
She reigns beside the waters yet in pride.
Rude voices cry: but in her ears the chime
Of full sad bells brings back her old springtide.

Like to a queen in pride of place, she wears
The splendour of a crown in Radcliffe's dome.
Well fare she – well! As perfect beauty fares,
And those high places that are beauty's home.

LIONEL JOHNSON (1867–1902)

Johnson recalled one 'whose crystal lips Athenian speech recall'
etc. This was Cardinal Newman. Johnson, in a characteristically
1890s dualism, combined fervent Roman Catholicism with
the life of a Soho drunk. In this poem, Ezra Pound speaks of
Johnson's death:

## FROM Hugh Selwyn Mauberley

Among the pickled foetuses and bottled bones,
Engaged in perfecting the catalogue,
I found the last scion of the
Senatorial families of Strasbourg, Monsieur Verog.

For two hours he talked of Gallifet;
Of Dowson; of the Rhymers' Club;
Told me how Johnson (Lionel) died
By falling from a high stool in a pub . . .

But showed no trace of alcohol
At the autopsy, privately performed –
Tissue preserved – the pure mind
Arose toward Newman as the whisky warmed.

Dowson found harlots cheaper than hotels;
Headlam for uplift; Image impartially imbued
With raptures for Bacchus, Terpischore and the Church.
So spoke the author of 'The Dorian Mood',

M. Verog, out of step with the decade,
Detached from his contemporaries,
Neglected by the young,
Because of these reveries.

 EZRA POUND (1885–1972)

# EIGHT

# THE PEOPLE OF ENGLAND

England is no more, but the people of England remain. G. K. Chesterton wrote his great poem 'The Secret People' nearly a hundred years ago. Now that they no longer truly have a home to go to, the silence of the English seems more potent, their rage more justified.

## The Secret People

Smile at us, pay us, pass us; but do not quite forget;
For we are the people of England, that never have spoken yet.
There is many a fat farmer that drinks less cheerfully,
There is many a free French peasant who is richer and
                                        sadder than we.
There are no folk in the whole world so helpless or so wise.
There is hunger in our bellies, there is laughter in our eyes;
You laugh at us and love us, both mugs and eyes are wet:
Only you do not know us. For we have not spoken yet.

The fine French kings came over in a flutter of flags and dames.
We liked their smiles and battles, but we never could
                                        say their names.
The blood ran red to Bosworth and the high French
                                        lords went down;
There was naught but a naked people under a naked crown.

And the eyes of the King's Servants turned terribly
                                    every way,
And the gold of the King's Servants rose higher every day.
They burnt the homes of the shaven men, that had
                                    been quaint and kind,
Till there was no bed in a monk's house, nor food that
                                    man could find.
The inns of God where no man paid, that were the wall
                                    of the weak,
The King's Servants ate them all. And still we did not speak.

And the face of the King's Servants grew greater than
                                    the King:
He tricked them, and they trapped him, and stood
                                    round him in a ring.
The new grave lords closed round him, that had eaten
                                    the abbey's fruits,
And the men of the new religion, with their bibles in
                                    their boots,
We saw their shoulders moving, to menace or discuss,
And some were pure and some were vile; but none took
                                    heed of us.
We saw the King as they killed him, and his face was
                                    proud and pale;
And a few men talked of freedom, while England talked
                                    of ale.

A war that we understood not came over the world and woke
Americans, Frenchmen, Irish; but we knew not the things
                                    they spoke.
They talked about rights and nature and peace and
                                    the people's reign:

And the squires, our masters, bade us fight; and scorned
us never again.
Weak if we be for ever, could none condemn us then;
Men called us serfs and drudges; men knew that we
were men.
In foam and flame at Trafalgar, on Albuera plains,
We did and died like lions, to keep ourselves in chains
We lay in living ruins; firing and fearing not
The strange fierce face of the Frenchmen who knew
for what they fought,
And the man who seemed to be more than man we
strained against and broke;
And we broke our own rights with him. And still we
never spoke.

Our patch of glory ended; we never heard guns again.
But the squire seemed struck in the saddle; he was
foolish, as if in pain.
He leaned on a staggering lawyer, he clutched a cringing Jew,
He was stricken; it may be, after all, he was stricken
at Waterloo.
Or perhaps the shades of the shaven men, whose spoil
is in his house,
Come back in shining shapes at last to spoil his last carouse:
We only know the last sad squires ride slowly towards
the sea,
And a new people takes the land: and still it is not we.

They have given us into the hand of new unhappy lords,
Lords without anger and honour, who dare not carry
their swords.
They fight by shuffling papers; they have bright dead
alien eyes;

They look at our labour and laughter as a tired man
                                        looks at flies.
And the load of their loveless pity is worse than the
                                        ancient wrongs,
Their doors are shut in the evening; and they know
                                        no songs.

We hear men speaking for us of new laws strong and sweet,
Yet is there no man speaketh as we speak in the street.
It may be we shall rise the last as Frenchmen rose the first,
Our wrath come after Russia's wrath and our wrath
                                        be the worst.
It may be we are meant to mark with our riot and our rest
God's score for all men governing. It may be beer is best.
But we are the people of England; and we have not
                                        spoken yet.
Smile at us, pay us, pass us. But do not quite forget.

G. K. CHESTERTON (1874–1936)

We should end with a bang, and not a whimper. In this section, I have gathered together some poems of protest. They are all written at different times. Some are politically left wing, others of the right. They boil with the sense of the people of England being let down by their governors. Ernest Jones was born in Germany and his first job was as courtier to William, Duke of Cumberland. But coming to England, Jones was radicalised and became an ardent champion of the cause of every man in England having the vote. For his part in Chartist demonstrations in Manchester he suffered two years' solitary confinement – time usefully spent composing the epic 'The Revolt of Hindostan'. Here is his 'The Song of the Low', with its refrain:

> We're low – we're low – we're very very low,
>   As low as low can be;
> The rich are high – for we make them so –
>   And a miserable lot are we!
>   And a miserable lot are we! are we!
>     A miserable lot are we!

## The Song of the Low

> We plough and sow – we're so very, very low
>   That we delve in the dirty clay,
> Till we bless the plain with the golden grain,
>   And the vale with the fragrant hay.
> Our place we know – we're so very low,
>   'Tis down at the landlord's feet:
> We're not too low the bread to grow,
>   But too low the bread to eat.
>     *We're low – we're low – etc.*

Down, down we go – we're so very low,
    To the hell of the deep sunk mines,
But we gather the proudest gems that glow,
    When the crown of a despot shines.
And whenever he lacks, upon our backs
    Fresh loads he deigns to lay:
We're far too low to vote the tax,
    But not too low to pay.
        *We're low – we're low – etc.*

We're low – we're low – mere rabble, we know,
    But, at our plastic power,
The mould at the lordling's feet will grow
    Into palace and church and tower.
Then prostrate fall in the rich man's hall,
    And cringe at the rich man's door:
We're not too low to build the wall,
    But too low to tread the floor.
        *We're low – we're low – etc.*

We're low – we're low – we're very, very low,
    Yet from our fingers glide
The silken flow – and the robes that glow
    Round the limbs of the sons of pride.
And what we get – and what we give –
    We know, and we know our share:
We're not too low the cloth to weave,
    But too low the cloth to wear!
        *We're low – we're low – etc.*

We're low – we're low – we're very, very low,
    And yet when the trumpets ring,
The thrust of a poor man's arm will go
    Thro' the heart of the proudest king.

We're low – we're low – our place we know,
    We're only the rank and file,
We're not too low to kill the foe,
    But too low to touch the spoil.
         *We're low – we're low – etc.*

ERNEST JONES (1819–69)

Percy Bysshe Shelley was not merely one of the finest lyricists in English. He was also one of England's most impassioned radicals who abominated 'an old, mad, blind, despised and dying king' – ie. George III – and the corrupt government. His 'Song to the Men of England' was written in 1819, the year before the King died.

## Song to the Men of England

### 1

Men of England, wherefore plough
For the lords who lay ye low?
Wherefore weave with toil and care
The rich robes your tyrants wear?

### 2

Wherefore feed, and clothe, and save,
From the cradle to the grave,
Those ungrateful drones who would
Drain your sweat – nay, drink your blood?

### 3

Wherefore, Bees of England, force
Many a weapon, chain and scourge.

That these stingless drones may spoil
The forced produce of your toil?

### 4

Have ye leisure, comfort, calm,
Shelter, food, love's gentle balm?
Or what is it ye buy so dear
With your pain and with your fear?

### 5

The seed ye sow, another reaps;
The wealth ye find, another keeps;
The robes ye weave, another wears;
The arms ye forge, another bears.

### 6

Sow seed,– but let no tyrant reap;
Find wealth,– let no impostor keep;
Weave robes,– let not the idle wear;
Forge arms,– in your defence to bear.

### 7

Shrink to your cellars, holes, and cells;
In halls ye deck another dwells.
Why shake the chains ye wrought? Ye see
The steel ye tempered glance on ye.

### 8

With plough and spade, and hoe and loom,
Trace your grave, and build your tomb,
And weave your winding-sheet, till fair
England be your sepulchre.

PERCY BYSSHE SHELLEY (1792–1822)

The Muses did not only smile upon leftists – witness the careers of Celine, of Knut Hamsun or of T. S. Eliot. Few careers in the history of literature, however, have been odder than that of Lord Alfred Douglas, a man whose reputation as a sonneteer has been overshadowed by his colourful personality. In his youth, his fey beauty led to the ruin of Oscar Wilde. Though a serious and ambitious poet, his reputation as a litigious and quarrelsome man, in temperament not unlike his choleric father the Scarlet Marquess of Queensberry, diminished the seriousness with which he was regarded by critics. He squeezed opinions of the most intemperate kind into the sonnet form. 'The leprous spawn of scattered Israel/Spreads its contagion in your English blood!' he expostulated in 1905. He was sued for libel by Winston Churchill, but came round to his old enemy during the Second World War – 'Not that of old I loved you over-much' . . . 'Like your sire/You rode the whirlwind and outstormed the storm'. In 1941, Bosie was a bottle-nosed old man, living with a farmer and his wife in Sussex. The old school tie to which allusion is made in the sonnet is that of Winchester. He died in 1945, four years after writing this, lying on his bed and clutching his latest betting slips – for he remained an incurable gambler.

## The Old Soldier

I say my prayers and wear my old school tie,
I was for Franco in the Spanish war.
I cherish peace but never took the floor
In favour of disarmament, I try
Not to forget that self-sufficiency
Was England's motto in the days before
The idiot 'League'. But doubtless I'm a bore
And sheer anathema to Bloomsbury.

I never would have crawled before Sinn Fein,
Or licked the boots of 'Dev'; I thought with Foch
About Versailles. I rate hell's murkiest imp
Above a pacifist. I'd say again
All that I said about the unchanging 'Boche'.
But then, of course, I'm only Colonel Blimp.

LORD ALFRED DOUGLAS (1870–1945)

Jonathan Trelawney was the Bishop of Bristol in 1688, and he was one of the seven bishops committed to the Tower of London by James II for refusing to accept that monarch's high-handed imposition of Roman Catholicism on English institutions such as the universities. The trial and acquittal of the seven bishops led to a great popular uprising, nowhere more than in Cornwall, where Trelawney was born at Pelynt, and where he is buried. It was another great Cornish eccentric, Stephen Hawker, who immortalised the popular ballad and made it into the present poem. It is much more than a poem about one abuse of power by a long-dead monarch. Ever since it was first sung, it has been a celebration of that cussedness, and that refusal to be bossed, which has been one of the glories of the English people. Describing the end of the Second World War, A. J. P. Taylor said, 'Few now sang, "Land of Hope and Glory". Few even sang "England Arise". England had risen all the same.' They were optimistic words written over forty years ago. Though England as an entity has been extinguished, the people who live there, and not just the Cornish, can, it is hoped, still unite one day to defy the 'gentlemen who know best' with the words – 'Come forth, come forth, ye cowards all/here's men as good as you!'

# The Song of the Western Men

A good sword and a trusty hand!
  A merry heart and true!
King James's men shall understand
  What Cornish lads can do.

And have they fix'd the where and when?
  And shall Trelawney die?
Here's twenty thousand Cornish men
  Will know the reason why!

Out spake their Captain brave and bold,
  A merry wight was he;
'If London Tower were Michael's Hold,
  We'll set Trelawney free!

'We'll cross the Tamar, land to land,
  The Severn is no stay;
With "One and All" and hand to hand
  And who shall bid us nay?

'And when we come to London Wall,
  A pleasant sight to view,
Come forth, come forth, ye cowards all!
  Here's men as good as you.

'Trelawney he's in keep and hold,
  Trelawney he may die:
But here's twenty thousand Cornish bold
  Will know the reason why.'

*And shall Trelawney die?*
  *And shall Trelawney die?*
*Here's twenty thousand Cornish men*
  *Will know the reason why!*

R. S. HAWKER (1803–75)

# Acknowledgements

We would like to thank all of the authors for making this collection possible by allowing us to use their material, and gratefully acknowledge permission to reprint copyright material as follows:

PFD on behalf of the Estate of Hilaire Belloc for permission to use 'Ha'nacker Mill' and 'The Garden Party'; The Society of Authors for permission to use 'For the Fallen' by Laurence Binyon; the Estate of John Betjeman for permission to use 'Middlesex', 'Death of King George V', 'Executive', 'Harvest Hymn' and lines from 'A Lincolnshire Church'; David Higham Associates for permission to use 'Birmingham' by Louis Mac-Neice; the Estate of James MacGibbon for permission to use 'O Happy Dogs of England' by Stevie Smith; Penguin Books Ltd. for permission to quote from Brideshead Revisited by Evelyn Waugh; Geoffrey Hill and Houghton Mifflin Harcourt for permission to use 'The Herefordshire Carol' by Geoffrey Hill; Faber & Faber for permission to reprint 'Thank You, Fog' and 'Oxford' by W. H. Auden, 'Going, Going' by Philip Larkin, material from 'Little Gidding' by T. S. Eliot and lines from 'Hugh Selwyn Mauberley' by Ezra Pound.

Every effort has been made to trace or contact copyright holders. The publishers would be pleased to rectify any omissions brought to their notice at the earliest opportunity.

# Index of first lines

A good sword and a trusty hand! 107
Among the pickled foetuses and bottled bones 95
And did those feet in ancient time 72
As I went down to Dymchurch Wall 58
Cold eyelids that hide like a jewel 52
Don Juan, now saw Albion's earliest beauties 37
First come I: my name is Jowett 56
First drink a health, this solemn night 33
Gaily into Ruislip Gardens 22
Good night to the Season! 'Tis over! 61
Greyly tremendous the thunder 70
Grown used to New York weather 41
How vainly men themselves amaze 45
I am a young executive. No cuffs than mine are cleaner 81
I say my prayers and wear my old school tie 105
I thought it would last my time 83
If I should die, think only this of me 17
If you came this way 87
Last night, among his fellow roughs 35
Men of England, wherefore plough 103
Methinks I am a prophet new inspir'd 11
Milton! Thou shouldst be living at this hour 80
Most gracious God, we humbly beseech thee . . . 76
Nature invades: old rooks in each college garden 92
O happy dogs of England 67
O to be in England 44
O valiant hearts who to your glory came 18
On forelands high in heaven 70
On Wenlock Edge the wood's in trouble 25
Once more unto the breach, dear friends, once more 32

One evening when his ferret strayed  88

Outside the garden  53

Over the four long years! And now there rings  93

Ralph and Jos (I, He) humble, poor, and lowly born  75

Sally is gone that was so kindly  16

Satire, be kind, and draw a silent veil  9

See you the ferny ride that steals  14

Smile at us, pay us, pass us; but do not quite forget  97

Smoke from the train-gulf hid by hoardings blunders upward,
    the brakes of cars  90

So to celebrate that kingdom: it grows  49

Spirits of well-shot woodcock, partridge, snipe  77

That night your great guns, unawares  20

The even oer the meadow seems to stoop  50

The Rich arrived in pairs  85

The sea is calm to-night  73

The stately Homes of England  65

There the ash-tree leaves do vall  59

There's a breathless hush in the Close to-night  31

Thy forests, Windsor! and thy green retreats  43

To my true king I offered free from stain  69

We live long in our family and marry late  24

We plough and sow – we're so very, very low  101

We spray the fields and scatter  82

When rosy plumelets tuft the larch  51

When the British warrior Queen  29

With lifted feet, hands still  56

With proud thanksgiving, a mother for her children  19

Yes, I remember Adlestrop  13

# Index of poem titles

Adlestrop  13
Birmingham  90
Boadicea  29
Brideshead Revisited, *from*
    24
Channel Firing  20
Death of King George V  77
Dolores (Notre Dame des
    Sept Douleurs), *from* 52
Don Juan, *from*  37
Dover Beach  73
England 1802, *from*  80
Executive  81
For the Fallen  19
Garden, The  45
Garden Party, The  85
Going down Hill on a
    Bicycle  56
Going, Going  83
Good Night to the Season  61
Ha'nacker Mill  16
Hands All Round!  33
Harvest Hymn  82
Henry V, *from*  32
Herefordshire Carol, The  49
HMS Pinafore, *from*  75
Homes of England, The  65
Home-thoughts, from
    Abroad  44
Hugh Selwyn Mauberley,
    *from* 95
In Memoriam, 51

In Romney Marsh  58
Jacobite's Epitaph, A  69
Jerusalem  72
Leaves a-Vallen  59
Lincolnshire Church, A, *from*  70
Little Gidding, *from*  87
Middlesex  22
Mist in the Meadows  50
O Happy Dogs of England  67
O Valiant Hearts  18
Old Soldier, The  105
Oxford  92, 93
Prayer for the High Court of
    Parliament, A  76
Private of the Buffs, The  35
Puck of Pook's Hill, *from*  14
Richard II, *from*  11
Roman Villa, A  88
Secret People, The  97
Shropshire Lad, A, *from*  25
Soldier, The  17
Song of the Low, The  101
Song of the Western Men,
    The  107
Song to the Men of England  103
Thank You, Fog  41
True-Born Englishman, The,
    *from* 9
Vitaï Lampada  31
Windsor-Forest, *from*  43
Winter in Northumberland,
    *from*  53

# Index of poets

Arkwright, Sir John  18
Arnold, Matthew  73
Auden, W. H.  41, 92
Barnes, William  59
Beeching, Henry Charles  56
Belloc, Hilaire  16, 85
Betjeman, John  22, 70, 77,
    81, 82
Binyon, Laurence  19
Blake, William  72
Brooke, Rupert  17
Browning, Robert  44
Byron, Lord  37
Chesterton, G. K.  97
Clare, John  50
Cowper, William  29
Cranmer, Thomas  76
Davidson, John  58
Defoe, Daniel  9
Douglas, Lord Alfred  105
Doyle, Sir Francis Hastings
    35
Eliot, T. S.  87
Falkner, J. M.  88
Gilbert, W. S.  75

Hardy, Thomas  20
Hawker, R. S.  107
Hemans, Felicia  65
Hill, Geoffrey  49
Housman, A. E.  25, 70
Johnson, Lionel  93
Jones, Ernest  101
Kipling, Rudyard  14
Larkin, Philip  83
Macaulay, Thomas Babington
    69
MacNeice, Louis  90
Marvell, Andrew  45
Newbolt, Henry  31
Pope, Alexander  43
Pound, Ezra  95
Praed, W. M.  61
Shakespeare, William  11, 32
Shelley, Percy Bysshe  103
Smith, Stevie  67
Swinburne, A. C.  52, 53
Tennyson, Alfred, Lord  33,
    51
Thomas, Edward  13
Waugh, Evelyn  24
Wordsworth, William  80